AF433964

Tickled to Death
Funny Epitaphs
For Kids

Jon Coley

While every precaution has been taken in the preparation of this book, the publisher assumes no responsibility for errors or omissions, or for damages resulting from the use of the information contained herein.

TICKLED TO DEATH: FUNNY EPITAPHS FOR KIDS

First edition. May 8, 2023.

ISBN: 979-8223829676

Written by Jon Coley.

Epitaphs are poems written on the grave stones of our beloved deceased. While visiting an amusement park with a famous rodent mascot, I noticed some funny epitaphs written on grave markers. It was on my favorite ride, THE HAUNTED MANSION.

This collection of poetry is meant to make you laugh, much the same way those epitaphs made me laugh while waiting in line. The names in each poem aren't actually related to real persons.

I teach school, and decided to use some of the names on the class rosters. Rest assured, this is all in good fun. I do not fantasize on my students' untimely demise. Usually.

Welcome to Our
Graveyard
Our Residents are
Tickled to Death to
Have You Here
Enjoy the Tour

Here Lies Eli
Who Slipped on a Cow Pie
And Why is He Now Dead?
Well, He Landed on His
Head

Rest In Peace Laynee
You Were so Sweet and
Never Dull
As Smart as You had been,
Now Worms Wiggle in
Your Skull

Here Lies Gibson
Who Robbed a Bank in Lisbon
He Jumped From The Plane With
all Of His Loot
If Only He'd Remembered That
Darned Parachute

Here Lies Jillian
A Friend to All of Us
She Should Have
Looked Both Ways
Before Walking in
Front of that Bus

Rest In Peace Logan
Who Engaged in Battle
with a Shogun
And how Sad it was
When He Died
For Out Came What
Should've Stayed Inside

Our Dearest Camryn
To Live on the Lake was Her
Greatest of Wishes
Hard She Worked All Her Life
Now She is Sleeping
with the Fishes

Here Lies Young Carson
Who Had a Long Career of
Theft and Arson
He Stole a Car
for Goodness Sakes
Too Bad it Didn't Have
any Brakes

Rest In Peace Gabriel
Born with the Gift Of Gab
It's a Shame You Opened
the Wrong Door
Into the Pathogen Lab

Here Lies Kaylee
Who Was Never A Phony
Still She Should Not
Have Eaten
That Expired Pepperoni

Here Lies Talon
Our Good Friend And Brother
His Body Went One Way
But His Head Went the Other

Rest In Peace Riley
An Outgoing Super Star
Until That Day in the Cannery
She was Stuffed in a Pickle Jar

Here Lies Adeline
Born With the Gift of Snark
But That Didn't Help Her One
Bit
When She Was Attacked by
That Shark

Rest In Peace Dayton
Oh How You Fought it
But You Were Down with the
Sickness
Since the Day You First
Caught it

Here Lies Evie
Who Played Sports
Like She Was Taught
But that Softball to the Face
Was Harder
Than She Thought

Rest In Peace Ileigh
While Looking For Gum That
Was Secretly Stashed
She Was Driving Her Car
And That's Why it Crashed

Rest In Peace Jenna
A Lover of Music
It Was Always Said
But She Did Not Love It
at All
When a Piano Fell
on Her Head

Here Lies Bryson
Renowned Social Media Poster
Who Shouldn't Have Been
Bathing
While Warming Bread with a
Toaster

Rest In Peace Jayce
Who Couldn't have felt
dumber
He Went to See a Doctor
Who Was Really Only a
Plumber

Here Lies Eliga
By the Lake
They Threw the Ball to Him
He Was a Masterful Catcher
But Did Not Know
How to Swim

Rest In Peace Alexa
We Thought You Were Playing
a Trick
That's Why Your Last Words
Were
"See? I Told You I Was Sick"

Our Dearest Emma
Who Felt Quite Like a Buffoon,
For She Ran Out of Gas
In Her Hot Air Balloon

Here Lies Landon
Who Thought
His Catch Was the Best
Until He Discovered That
Swordfish in His Chest

Rest In Peace Xander
Whose Situation Was Dire
For Someone
Flipped a Switch
While He Was Holding
That Wire

Hear lies Hunter
Who Could Sometimes
Be Dense
After All We Did
Warn Him
Not to Pee
on That Electric Fence

Rest In Peace Micah
Who Got Into a Tangle
When His Little Boat Sailed
Into the Bermuda Triangle

Here Lies Mackenzye
Who was Solid Rock Steady
But as Stable as She Was,
Her House Wasn't
Earthquake Ready

Rest In Peace Cody
Well, What Do I Know?
Perhaps it was not
Such a Good Idea
To Mess With That Grumpy
Rhino

Here lies Raven
Who Just Wasn't Listening
When We Told Him
That Crate
Was Filled With
Nitroglycerin

Rest In Peace Tatum
It Was Such a Shame
Learning That Those Two Things
Don't Go Together
Hairspray and a Flame

Here Lies Reagan
Who Thought
She Knew it All
But Didn't Understand
What Happens When Your
Car Collides
With a Wall

Rest In Peace Braylin
Who Spoke Up
at His Tribunal
Even Though His Lawyer
Advised If You Do So,
It's Your Funeral

Here Lies Rivers
Who Lived Life
Without a Care
But He Definitely
Had a Few Worries
When He Stepped On That
Sleeping Bear

Rest In Peace Gabi
You Had Long,
Beautiful Hair
Too Bad You Didn't See
That Running
Wood Chipper Over There

Here lies Blakelynn
Who Enjoyed
The Shooting Range
But When Asked To Hold
the Target
She Thought That
Was a Little Strange

Rest In Peace Callein
Who Invented a
Lighter Bulletproof Vest
He Wore it Proudly,
However,
It Did Not Pass the Test

Here lies Braden
He Enjoyed
Tempting the Fates
Alas it Would Seem
That a Rooftop
Is Not Where One
Should Wear Roller Skates

Rest In Peace Sawyer
Who Was Mad as a Red Blister
For He Began Work
in a Knife Factory
The Day It Was Hit by a Twister

Here Lies Ray
As a Tailor
He Was the Greatest of Wizards
Too Bad His Mother
Didn't Teach Him
Never to Run Around
With Scissors

Rest In Peace Mollie
You Thought the Hippo Was
So Cute
But After Crunching
Your Head Like a Melon
It Let Out
a Disgusting Poot

Here Lies Gavin
Whose Heart
Was Quite Tender
Especially After Tripping
and Falling
Into an Industrial Blender

Rest In Peace Ny'Asia
A Dedicated Army Mom
She Should've Cut
the Red Wire
While She Was
Diffusing That Bomb

Here Lies Chance
Whose Condition
Did Suddenly Worsen
He Forgot
He Wasn't on the Internet
And Said the Wrong Thing to
the Wrong Person

Rest In Peace Addy
Who Was Fond of
The Shovel and Rake
Unfortunately
She Had Neither on Hand
When She Stepped
On That Rattlesnake

Rest In Peace Xara
Lover of Hiking
And Keeping Notes
in a Binder
The Last Line She Wrote in it Was
Hey, I Think I See A Sidewinder!

Here Lies Xaria
Quite Proud of Her
Psychic Prowess
When Turning a Corner
the Puma Attacked
Her Last Words Were,
"Who Could Have Guessed?"

Rest in Peace Corbin
A Video Game
He Was Determined to Beat
For Weeks He Was
Locked in His Room
Turned Out
He Had Nothing to Eat

Here Lies Nikiita
Who Worked on
A Power Line Truck
As Her Bucket Was Falling
She Knew
She Was Plain Out of Luck

Rest In Peace Taziyah
She Liked Playing The Clown
That's Why She Fell Overboard
Whereupon
She Unfortunately Drowned.

McKenzie
She Sought Vengeance
for Logan
She Ended Up
Just Like Him
That Was One
Dangerous Shogun

Here Lies Madalyn
Obsessed She Was
With Ghosts
It's All Too Ironic
She Became What
Fascinated Her Most

Rest In Peace Colton
A Mountain Climber, Strong
And Slim
He Did Not fall Off a Cliff
Some of it Fell on Him

Here Lies Cadee
There's No Need To Roast
Her.
She Didn't
Buckle Her Seatbelt
Before Riding
the Roller Coaster

Rest in Peace Lilly
There is No Need
To Be Mean
Still, She Had to
Know in Her Heart
Raw Egg Yolks
Are Never Green

Here Lies Nathan
He Wasn't
Making a Peep
Finally We All Realized
He Died Quietly
In His Sleep

Rest in Peace Marcus
He Ran
Super Fast
Around the Track
No Doubt He
Felt Like a Winner
Until
He Had That Heart Attack

Our Dearest EmaLee
All That's Left is a Stain
But That's What
Always Happens
When You Get Hit
By a Train

Here Lies Jeremy
He Was Quite
Insane, Though
That is Why
He Had No Worries
When He Climbed
That Active Volcano

About the Author

Jon Coley lives in Georgia with his wife, daughters, and orange cat, and an eccentric husky.

Other books for kids by Jon Coley

THE CURSE OF MR. M'S CASTLE
THE OTHER CURSE OF MR. M'S CASTLE
ALL GRANDPAS FISH
SKATE OR DIE JACOB JONES
THE BOOKWORM
THE FISH CREEK FORUM: VOLUME 1
WAS THAT SUPPOSED TO BE FUNNY?
CHUCKLE WORTHY JOKES FOR KIDS
WAS THAT SOME KIND OF JOKE? FUNNY
JOKES FOR KIDS
LIMERICK CITY: FUNNY POEMS FOR KIDS

Contacts:

www.joncoleyauthor.com

facebook.com/Jon Coley Author

www.Amazon.com/author/joncoley

Instagram @JonColeyAuthor

Thank you for reading this book. If you enjoyed it, please consider giving it a rating and review.

Thanks!

Here Lies Jeremy
He Was Quite
Insane, Though
That is Why
He Had No Worries
When He Climbed
That Active Volcano

About the Author

Jon Coley lives in Georgia with his wife, daughters, and orange cat, and an eccentric husky.

Other books for kids by Jon Coley

THE CURSE OF MR. M'S CASTLE
THE OTHER CURSE OF MR. M'S CASTLE
ALL GRANDPAS FISH
SKATE OR DIE JACOB JONES
THE BOOKWORM
THE FISH CREEK FORUM: VOLUME 1
WAS THAT SUPPOSED TO BE FUNNY?
CHUCKLE WORTHY JOKES FOR KIDS
WAS THAT SOME KIND OF JOKE? FUNNY
JOKES FOR KIDS
LIMERICK CITY: FUNNY POEMS FOR KIDS

Contacts:

www.joncoleyauthor.com

facebook.com/Jon Coley Author

Instagram @JonColeyAuthor

www.ingramcontent.com/pod-product-compliance
Lightning Source LLC
Chambersburg PA
CBHW031801150726
47989CB00006B/2829